MY SUMMER CAMP JOURNAL FOR KIDS

D1075903

MY Awesome SUMMER

YEAR

THIS JOURNAL BELONGS TO:

I AM ----------------- YEARS OLD

THIS IS ME

Camp Info

Camp Name: _____

Location: _____

This is my _____ year of camp.

How I'm feeling about camp...

_____

_____

_____

_____

_____

_____

Packing List

Make a list of all the things you want to bring with you to camp. Check the smiley face box as you pack each item.

As you get ready to come home, check the box with a house as you pack each item.

Packing List

Make a list of all the things you want to bring with you to camp. Check the smiley face box as you pack each item.

As you get ready to come home, check the box with a house as you pack each item.

Addresses
to remember to write home

Name: _____

Address: _____

_____

Phone: _____

Email: _____

Name: _____

Address: _____

_____

Phone: _____

Email: _____

Name: _____

Address: _____

_____

Phone: _____

Email: _____

Addresses

to remember to write home

Name: _____

Address: _____

_____

Phone: _____

Email: _____

Name: _____

Address: _____

_____

Phone: _____

Email: _____

Name: _____

Address: _____

_____

Phone: _____

Email: _____

Message From Home

Your family can fill this out before you leave.

_____

_____

_____

_____

_____

_____

_____

_____

_____

_____

_____

_____

_____

_____

_____

_____

Nature Scavenger HUNT

How many can you find? Take your time!

- [ ] Something colorful
- [ ] A flower or petal
- [ ] Something bumpy
- [ ] A flat rock
- [ ] Something spiky
- [ ] Something that makes noise
- [ ] An insect
- [ ] Something rough
- [ ] Something round
- [ ] Two kinds of leaves
- [ ] Something with a hole in it
- [ ] Something scented
- [ ] Something triangle shaped

- [ ] Something thin
- [ ] A spider web
- [ ] A feather
- [ ] Something soft
- [ ] Something patterned
- [ ] A seed
- [ ] Something pretty
- [ ] A long and a short stick
- [ ] Something small
- [ ] A bird
- [ ] Litter (throw it away)
- [ ] A piece of bark
- [ ] Treasure (to you)

Draw a map of camp

Draw where you sleep

Camp Speak

WRITE DOWN ANY FUNNY QUOTES, SONG LYRICS, OR
CAMP LINGO YOU WANT TO REMEMBER.

Camp Speak

WRITE DOWN ANY FUNNY QUOTES, SONG LYRICS, OR
CAMP LINGO YOU WANT TO REMEMBER.

Daily Journal

Date:_____ Su M T W Th F S

Weather

3 things I did today...

1 _____

2 _____

3 _____

Best food I ate today:

Highlight of the day!

_____

_____

_____

_____

Rate Your Day: ☆ ☆ ☆ ☆ ☆

Daily Journal

Date:_____ Su M T W Th F S

Weather

3 things I did today...

1 _____

2 _____

3 _____

Best food I ate today:

Highlight of the day!

_____

_____

_____

_____

Rate Your Day: ☆ ☆ ☆ ☆ ☆

Daily Journal

Date: _____ (Su) (M) (T) (W) (Th) (F) (S)

Weather

3 things I did today...

1 _____

2 _____

3 _____

Best food I ate today:

Highlight of the day!

_____

_____

_____

_____

Rate Your Day: ☆ ☆ ☆ ☆ ☆

Daily Journal

Date:_____ Su M T W Th F S

Weather

3 things I did today...

1 _____

2 _____

3 _____

Best food I ate today:

Highlight of the day!

_____

_____

_____

_____

Rate Your Day: ☆ ☆ ☆ ☆ ☆

Daily Journal

Date:_____ Su M T W Th F S

Weather

3 things I did today...

1 --

2 --

3 --

Best food I ate today:

Highlight of the day!

Rate Your Day: ☆ ☆ ☆ ☆ ☆

Daily Journal

Date:_____ (Su)(M)(T)(W)(Th)(F)(S)

Weather

3 things I did today...

1 _____

2 _____

3 _____

Best food I ate today:

Highlight of the day!

_____

_____

_____

_____

Rate Your Day: ☆ ☆ ☆ ☆ ☆

Daily Journal

Date:_____ (Su) (M) (T) (W) (Th) (F) (S)

Weather

3 things I did today...

1 ....

2 ....

3 ....

Best food I ate today:

Highlight of the day!

....

....

....

....

Rate Your Day:

Daily Journal

Date:_____ Su M T W Th F S

Weather

3 things I did today...

1 _____

2 _____

3 _____

Best food I ate today:

Highlight of the day!

_____

_____

_____

_____

Rate Your Day: ☆ ☆ ☆ ☆ ☆

Daily Journal

Date:_____ (Su)(M)(T)(W)(Th)(F)(S)

Weather

3 things I did today...

1 _____

2 _____

3 _____

Best food I ate today:

Highlight of the day!

_____

_____

_____

_____

Rate Your Day: ☆ ☆ ☆ ☆ ☆

Daily Journal

Date:_____ Su M T W Th F S

Weather

3 things I did today...

1 --

2 --

3 --

Best food I ate today:

Highlight of the day!

Rate Your Day: ☆ ☆ ☆ ☆ ☆

Daily Journal

Date:_____ (Su) (M) (T) (W) (Th) (F) (S)

Weather

3 things I did today...

1 ....

2 ....

3 ....

Best food I ate today:

Highlight of the day!

....

....

....

....

Rate Your Day: ☆ ☆ ☆ ☆ ☆

Daily Journal

Date:_____ Su M T W Th F S

Weather

3 things I did today...

1 --

2 --

3 --

Best food I ate today:

Highlight of the day!

Rate Your Day: ☆ ☆ ☆ ☆ ☆

Daily Journal

Date:_____ Su M T W Th F S

Weather

3 things I did today...

1 _____

2 _____

3 _____

Best food I ate today:

Highlight of the day!

_____

_____

_____

_____

Rate Your Day: ☆ ☆ ☆ ☆ ☆

Daily Journal

Date:_____ Su M T W Th F S

Weather

3 things I did today...

1 --

2 --

3 --

Best food I ate today:

Highlight of the day!

Rate Your Day:

Daily Journal

Date:_____ (Su)(M)(T)(W)(Th)(F)(S)

Weather

3 things I did today...

1 _____

2 _____

3 _____

Best food I ate today:

Highlight of the day!

_____

_____

_____

_____

Rate Your Day: ☆ ☆ ☆ ☆ ☆

Daily Journal

Date:_____ Su M T W Th F S

Weather

3 things I did today...

1 _____

2 _____

3 _____

Best food I ate today:

Highlight of the day!

_____

_____

_____

_____

Rate Your Day: ☆ ☆ ☆ ☆ ☆

Daily Journal

Date:_____ (Su)(M)(T)(W)(Th)(F)(S)

Weather

3 things I did today...

1. ------------------------------------
2. ------------------------------------
3. ------------------------------------

Best food I ate today:

Highlight of the day!

Rate Your Day: ☆ ☆ ☆ ☆ ☆

Daily Journal

Date:_____ Su M T W Th F S

Weather

3 things I did today...

1 --

2 --

3 --

Best food I ate today:

Highlight of the day!

Rate Your Day: ☆ ☆ ☆ ☆ ☆

Daily Journal

Date:_____ (Su)(M)(T)(W)(Th)(F)(S)

Weather

3 things I did today...

1 _____

2 _____

3 _____

Best food I ate today:

Highlight of the day!

_____

_____

_____

_____

Rate Your Day: ☆ ☆ ☆ ☆ ☆

Daily Journal

Date:_____ Su M T W Th F S

Weather

3 things I did today...

1 --
2 --
3 --

Best food I ate today:

Highlight of the day!

Rate Your Day: ☆ ☆ ☆ ☆ ☆

Daily Journal

Date:_____ (Su) (M) (T) (W) (Th) (F) (S)

Weather

3 things I did today...

1 --

2 --

3 --

Best food I ate today:

Highlight of the day!

Rate Your Day: ☆ ☆ ☆ ☆ ☆

Daily Journal

Date:_____ Su M T W Th F S

Weather

3 things I did today...

1. _____
2. _____
3. _____

Best food I ate today:

Highlight of the day!

_____
_____
_____
_____

Rate Your Day: ☆ ☆ ☆ ☆ ☆

Daily Journal

Date:_____ (Su) (M) (T) (W) (Th) (F) (S)

Weather

3 things I did today...

1 ....
2 ....
3 ....

Best food I ate today:

Highlight of the day!

....
....
....
....

Rate Your Day: ☆ ☆ ☆ ☆ ☆

Daily Journal

Date:_____ Su M T W Th F S

Weather

3 things I did today...

1 --

2 --

3 --

Best food I ate today:

Highlight of the day!

Rate Your Day: ☆ ☆ ☆ ☆ ☆

Daily Journal

Date:_____ (Su)(M)(T)(W)(Th)(F)(S)

Weather

3 things I did today...

1 --------------------------------

2 --------------------------------

3 --------------------------------

Best food I ate today:

Highlight of the day!

Rate Your Day: ☆ ☆ ☆ ☆ ☆

Daily Journal

Date:_____ Su M T W Th F S

Weather

3 things I did today...

1 --

2 --

3 --

Best food I ate today:

Highlight of the day!

Rate Your Day: ☆ ☆ ☆ ☆ ☆

Daily Journal

Date:_____ Su M T W Th F S

Weather

3 things I did today...

1 --

2 --

3 --

Best food I ate today:

Highlight of the day!

Rate Your Day:

Daily Journal

Date:_____ Su M T W Th F S

Weather

3 things I did today...

1 ....

2 ....

3 ....

Best food I ate today:

Highlight of the day!

....

....

....

....

Rate Your Day: ☆ ☆ ☆ ☆ ☆

Daily Journal

Date:_____ (Su) (M) (T) (W) (Th) (F) (S)

Weather

3 things I did today...

1 _____

2 _____

3 _____

Best food I ate today:

Highlight of the day!

_____

_____

_____

_____

Rate Your Day: ☆ ☆ ☆ ☆ ☆

Daily Journal

Date:_____ (Su) (M) (T) (W) (Th) (F) (S)

Weather

---

3 things I did today...

1 --
2 --
3 --

Best food I ate today:

Highlight of the day!

Rate Your Day:

Daily Journal

Date:_____ Su M T W Th F S

Weather

3 things I did today...

1. --
2. --
3. --

Best food I ate today:

Highlight of the day!

Rate Your Day: ☆ ☆ ☆ ☆ ☆

Daily Journal

Date:_____ (Su) (M) (T) (W) (Th) (F) (S)

Weather

3 things I did today...

1. _____
2. _____
3. _____

Best food I ate today:

Highlight of the day!

_____

_____

_____

_____

Rate Your Day: ☆ ☆ ☆ ☆ ☆

Daily Journal

Date:_____ (Su)(M)(T)(W)(Th)(F)(S)

Weather

3 things I did today...

1 ------------------------------------

2 ------------------------------------

3 ------------------------------------

Best food I ate today:

Highlight of the day!

Rate Your Day:

Daily Journal

Date:_____ Su M T W Th F S

Weather

3 things I did today...

1 --

2 --

3 --

Best food I ate today:

Highlight of the day!

Rate Your Day:

Daily Journal

Date:_____ (Su) (M) (T) (W) (Th) (F) (S)

Weather

3 things I did today...

1 _____

2 _____

3 _____

Best food I ate today:

Highlight of the day!

_____

_____

_____

_____

Rate Your Day: ☆ ☆ ☆ ☆ ☆

Daily Journal

Date:_____ Su M T W Th F S

Weather

3 things I did today...

1 --

2 --

3 --

Best food I ate today:

Highlight of the day!

Rate Your Day: ☆ ☆ ☆ ☆ ☆

Daily Journal

Date:_____ Su M T W Th F S

Weather

3 things I did today...

1 --

2 --

3 --

Best food I ate today:

Highlight of the day!

Rate Your Day: ☆ ☆ ☆ ☆ ☆

Daily Journal

Date:_____ (Su) (M) (T) (W) (Th) (F) (S)

Weather

3 things I did today...

1 --

2 --

3 --

Best food I ate today:

Highlight of the day!

Rate Your Day: ☆ ☆ ☆ ☆ ☆

Daily Journal

Date:_____ Su M T W Th F S

Weather

3 things I did today...

1 _____
2 _____
3 _____

Best food I ate today:

Highlight of the day!

_____
_____
_____
_____

Rate Your Day: ☆ ☆ ☆ ☆ ☆

Daily Journal

Date:_____ Su M T W Th F S

Weather

3 things I did today...

1 _____

2 _____

3 _____

Best food I ate today:

Highlight of the day!

_____

_____

_____

_____

Rate Your Day: ☆ ☆ ☆ ☆ ☆

Daily Journal

Date:_____ Su M T W Th F S

Weather

3 things I did today...

1 -
2 -
3 -

Best food I ate today:

Highlight of the day!

- -
- -
- -
- -

Rate Your Day: ☆ ☆ ☆ ☆ ☆

Daily Journal

Date:_____ (Su) (M) (T) (W) (Th) (F) (S)

Weather

3 things I did today...

1 --

2 --

3 --

Best food I ate today:

Highlight of the day!

Rate Your Day:

Daily Journal

Date:_____ (Su) (M) (T) (W) (Th) (F) (S)

Weather

3 things I did today...

1. --
2. --
3. --

Best food I ate today:

Highlight of the day!

Rate Your Day: ☆ ☆ ☆ ☆ ☆

Daily Journal

Date:_____ Su M T W Th F S

Weather

3 things I did today...

1 --
2 --
3 --

Best food I ate today:

Highlight of the day!

Rate Your Day: ☆ ☆ ☆ ☆ ☆

Daily Journal

Date:_____ Su M T W Th F S

Weather

3 things I did today...

1 _____
2 _____
3 _____

Best food I ate today:

Highlight of the day!

_____
_____
_____
_____

Rate Your Day: ☆ ☆ ☆ ☆ ☆

Daily Journal

Date:_____ Su M T W Th F S

Weather

3 things I did today...

1 --

2 --

3 --

Best food I ate today:

Highlight of the day!

Rate Your Day: ☆ ☆ ☆ ☆ ☆

Daily Journal

Date:_____ (Su) (M) (T) (W) (Th) (F) (S)

Weather

3 things I did today...

1 _____

2 _____

3 _____

Best food I ate today:

Highlight of the day!

_____

_____

_____

_____

Rate Your Day:

Daily Journal

Date:_____ (Su) (M) (T) (W) (Th) (F) (S)

Weather

3 things I did today...

1 --

2 --

3 --

Best food I ate today:

Highlight of the day!

Rate Your Day: ☆ ☆ ☆ ☆ ☆

Daily Journal

Date:_____ Su M T W Th F S

Weather

3 things I did today...

1 ....

2 ....

3 ....

Best food I ate today:

Highlight of the day!

....

....

....

....

Rate Your Day: ☆ ☆ ☆ ☆ ☆

Daily Journal

Date:_____ (Su) (M) (T) (W) (Th) (F) (S)

Weather

3 things I did today...

1. --
2. --
3. --

Best food I ate today:

Highlight of the day!

Rate Your Day:

Daily Journal

Date:_____ (Su) (M) (T) (W) (Th) (F) (S)

Weather

3 things I did today...

1 _____

2 _____

3 _____

Best food I ate today:

Highlight of the day!

_____

_____

_____

_____

Rate Your Day: ☆ ☆ ☆ ☆ ☆

Random Thoughts

Random Thoughts

Random Thoughts

Random Thoughts

New Friends

NAME: _____

Contact Info: _____

_____

_____

NAME: _____

Contact Info: _____

_____

_____

NAME: _____

Contact Info: _____

_____

_____

NAME: _____

Contact Info: _____

_____

_____

New Friends

NAME: _____
Contact Info: _____
_____
_____

NAME: _____
Contact Info: _____
_____
_____

NAME: _____
Contact Info: _____
_____
_____

NAME: _____
Contact Info: _____
_____
_____

New Friends

NAME: _____

Contact Info: _____

_____

_____

NAME: _____

Contact Info: _____

_____

_____

NAME: _____

Contact Info: _____

_____

_____

NAME: _____

Contact Info: _____

_____

_____

New Friends

NAME: _____
Contact Info: _____
_____
_____

NAME: _____
Contact Info: _____
_____
_____

NAME: _____
Contact Info: _____
_____
_____

NAME: _____
Contact Info: _____
_____
_____

My Awesome Counselors

AUTOGRAPHS

Thanks for the
Memories!

AUTOGRAPHS

Thanks for the
Memories!

AUTOGRAPHS

Thanks for the
Memories!

AUTOGRAPHS

Thanks for the
Memories!

And that's a wrap!

Would you come back to this camp?

☐ Yes ☐ No

The best part was...

The worst part was...

Camp Awards

Best Day: _____

Best Night: _____

Best Song: _____

Best Meal: _____

Best Counselor: _____

Best Weather: _____

Funniest Moment: _____

My Best Friends: _____

_____

Made in the USA
Monee, IL
08 July 2022